CHRISTMAS
— Cross-Stitch —
TREASURES

Joan Elliott

Introduction

Christmas is a most special time as the streets fill with the magic and sparkle of the holidays and a joyful spirit of hope and peace fills the air. Friends and family, sharing and giving indeed make this a most wonderful time of the year! Get a head start on your Christmas stitching with Joan Elliott's new treasury of Christmas designs that capture all the good cheer of the season.

Santa takes center stage as he soars above the rooftops on a spectacular magical reindeer. Loaded with toys and gifts, he starts on his annual journey around the world. Close to home, lilting carols are heard everywhere including the well-known "The Twelve Days of Christmas." Display a beautifully stitched wall hanging with colorful illustrations for each verse of this beloved song. In keeping with tradition, you will also find two quick and easy redwork samplers that will make the perfect gift for a holiday hostess.

Children always bring a special joy and wonder to Christmas. Imagine their delight when they see a special stocking overflowing with tiny surprises and made just for them. Choose from a darling fairy or a whimsical dragon and create a lasting treasure. Walk further into the realm of castles and enchantment with the elegant Snow Princess as she travels the snowy forest to greet her gentle subjects.

In the snowy north we find a charming group of snowmen making the most of the holiday festivities. Brightly colored decorations and sparkling light strings invite everyone to join in the fun. Add a personal touch to your holiday greetings with a set of four very merry designs worked in bright cheerful colors. Try using the same designs to create little gift bags that hold holiday sweets or a special token of affection. Round out your holiday stitching and decorate your tree with six lovable Christmas ornaments that will bring a smile to all.

All the designs in this book are quite straightforward to stitch. Beads and metallic threads bring an extra touch of holiday fun to your work. Not a fan of French knots? Try substituting petite glass beads instead. Add your own creativity with your choices of fabric and finishing. Happy stitching everyone!

Santa's Magical Journey,
page 4

The Twelve Days of Christmas,
page 10

Christmas Stockings,
page 16

The Snow Princess,
page 24

Meet the Designer

Joan Elliott has been creating needlework designs for close to 40 years. After graduating with a degree in Fine Arts, Joan's passion for color and interest in fiber art found an easy home in the needlework world. With countless cross-stitch designs to her credit, and more than 13 books of designs she has published over the years, her distinctive style is easily recognized and appreciated by cross-stitch fans around the world.

Joan's designs appear regularly in the major cross-stitch magazines in both the United States and the United Kingdom, and kits and chart packs of her designs are sold worldwide. Finding the enthusiasm of cross stitchers an inspiration, she loves keeping in touch with her fans through both her blog and Facebook page.

Joan always enjoys working on Christmas designs for cross-stitch and in this, her third book of all-new designs done exclusively for Annie's, she returns to bring the joy and festive spirit of Christmas to stitchers everywhere.

Joan divides her time between New York City and the peaceful countryside of Vermont where she joyfully indulges her passion for gardening and is forever inspired by the beauty of the nature that surrounds her. She and her husband feel truly blessed to share all the joys of both city and country life.

Redwork Christmas Samplers,
page 30

Snow Much Fun,
page 34

Christmas Greetings,
page 38

Christmas Roly-Polies,
page 42

Santa's Magical Journey

*Up and away on his magnificent reindeer,
Santa soars on his magical Christmas Eve
ride. With a twinkle in his eye and dressed
in his finest holiday cloak, he carries his
sack full of toys for children and a generous
spirit of joy to each and every home.*

Materials

- Cosmos 14- or 28-count Jobelan*:
  19 x 21 inches
- DMC floss as indicated in color key
- Kreinik Fine (#4) Braid as indicated in color key
- Mill Hill glass seed beads as indicated in color key

*Santa's Magical Journey was stitched on Cosmos 28-count hand-dyed
Jobelan from Polstitches Designs using DMC floss, Kreinik braid and
Mill Hill glass seed beads. Finished piece was custom framed.*

Skill Level
Experienced

Stitch Count
153 wide x 191 high

Approximate Design Size
11-count 14" x 17⅜"
14-count 11" x 13⅝"
16-count 9½" x 12"
18-count 8½" x 10⅝"
25-count 6⅛" x 7⅝"
28-count over 2 threads 11" x 13⅝"
32-count over 2 threads 9½" x 12"

Instructions
Center and stitch design on fabric using 2 strands
floss or 1 strand Kreinik braid for full, half and
quarter Cross-Stitch; 1 strand floss or Kreinik
braid for Backstitch; and 2 strands floss, wrapped
once, for French Knot. Attach beads using 1
strand matching floss.

FULL, HALF & QUARTER CROSS-STITCH (2X)

ANCHOR		DMC	COLORS
2	o	1	White
109	◇	155	Medium dark blue violet
399	⋘	318	Light steel gray
9046	♥	321	Red
119	✿	333	Very dark blue violet
398	e	415	Pearl gray
46	✤	666	Bright red
891	?	676	Light old gold
886	a	677	Very light old gold
923	♣	699	Green
227	∿	701	Light green
238	△	703	Chartreuse
890	▣	729	Medium old gold
303	★	742	Light tangerine
302	◕	743	Medium yellow
301	C	744	Pale yellow
132	✦	797	Royal blue
131	✳	798	Dark delft blue
136	⇨	799	Medium delft blue
944	←	869	Very dark hazelnut brown
381	●	938	Ultra dark coffee brown
881	⋈	945	Tawny
1010	√	951	Light tawny
73	♡	963	Ultra very light dusty rose
1030	✂	3746	Dark blue violet
1032	◣	3752	Very light antique blue
1031	<	3753	Ultra very light antique blue
1098	H	3801	Light red
901	◭	3829	Very dark old gold

FULL, HALF & QUARTER CROSS-STITCH (1X)

KREINIK VERY FINE (#4) BRAID		COLOR
028	m	Citron

BACKSTITCH (1X)

ANCHOR		DMC	COLORS
400	—	317	Pewter gray (Santa's beard, eye brow)
9046	—	321	Red*
381	—	938	Ultra dark coffee brown*

KREINIK VERY FINE (#4) BRAID		COLORS
025	—	Gray
028	—	Citron*

FRENCH KNOT (2X)

ANCHOR		DMC	COLORS
1	●	2	White* (reindeer's eye highlight)
381	●	938	Ultra dark coffee brown* (eyes on doll and bea

ATTACH BEAD

MILL HILL GLASS SEED		COLOR
G00557	●	Old gold

MILL HILL ANTIQUE SEED		COLOR
G03049	●	Rich red

*Duplicate color

The Twelve Days of Christmas

In the majestic halls and stately castles from a mythical time long ago, golden rings sparkled in holiday candlelight, lords and ladies celebrated the season, swans drifted peacefully in the still mountain lakes, and the pipers played a lilting holiday tune.

Materials

- Opalescent white 14- or 28-count Cashel linen: 16 x 31 inches
- DMC floss as indicated in color key
- Kreinik Fine (#4) Braid as indicated in color key
- Mill Hill glass seed beads as indicated in color key
- ¼ yard lightweight iron-on interfacing
- ½ yard banner fabric
- ½ yard fusible fleece
- ¼ yard fusible web
- 2 yards ¾-inch-wide decorative trim
- 4 winter-themed embellishments
- Permanent fabric glue
- 12-inch length ¾-inch wooden dowel

*The Twelve Days of Christmas was stitched on opalescent white 28-count hand-dyed Cashel linen from Polstitches Designs using DMC floss, Kreinik braid and Mill Hill glass seed beads.

Skill Level

Experienced

Stitch Count

111 wide x 323 high

Approximate Design Size

11-count 10" x 29⅜"
14-count 8" x 23"
16-count 7" x 20⅛"
18-count 6⅛" x 18"
25-count 4½" x 13"
28-count over 2 threads 8" x 23"
32-count over 2 threads 7" x 20⅛"

Project Note

Materials and finishing instructions are for banner stitched on 14-count fabric or on 28-count fabric over two threads.

Stitching

Center and stitch design on fabric using 2 strands floss or 1 strand Kreinik braid for full, half and quarter Cross-Stitch; 1 strand floss or Kreinik braid for Backstitch and Straight Stitch; and 2 strands floss, wrapped once, for French Knot. Attach beads using 1 strand matching floss.

Banner

Note: *Use ½-inch seam allowance throughout.*

1. Cut a 9 x 24-inch piece of iron-on interfacing and center it over the wrong side of the finished embroidery; fuse in place. Trim interfaced embroidery 7 rows beyond stitched design.
2. Cut 3 rectangles each 4 x 6 inches for hanging tabs. Fold each rectangle in half lengthwise, right sides together. Sew raw edges down the length and across one end. Trim seams, turn right side out and press.
3. Cut 2 pieces of banner fabric each 13 x 28 inches, and 1 piece of fusible fleece 13 x 28 inches. Fuse fleece to wrong side of 1 banner fabric piece. Place banner pieces right sides together, matching edges. Sandwich hanging tabs between layers, evenly spaced across the width of one end, with raw edges even. Sew banner edges, leaving an opening for turning. Turn right side out and press. Hand-stitch opening closed.
4. Place banner on work surface with fleece-backed side facing up. Cut a piece of fusible web the same size as the finished stitched piece, and then center the stitched piece on the banner with fusible web sandwiched between. Fuse according to the manufacturer's instructions.
5. Glue decorative trim carefully to the raw edge of the embroidery, starting and ending at center bottom. Sew 1 embellishment where the ends meet.
6. Bring ends of each tab to the front and attach to the banner by sewing. Glue an embellishment on each tab, referring to photo for placement.
7. To hang, insert wooden dowel through the tabs.

FULL, HALF & QUARTER CROSS-STITCH (2X)

ANCHOR	DMC	COLORS
2	1	White
109	155	Medium dark blue violet
403	310	Black
979	312	Very dark baby blue
399	318	Light steel gray
9046	321	Red
119	333	Very dark blue violet
977	334	Medium baby blue
13	349	Dark coral
10	351	Coral
398	415	Pearl gray
310	434	Light brown
1045	436	Tan
212	561	Very dark jade
210	562	Medium jade
891	676	Light old gold
228	700	Bright green
226	702	Kelly green

ANCHOR	DMC	COLORS
238	703	Chartreuse
890	729	Medium old gold
303	742	Light tangerine
302	743	Medium yellow
234	762	Very light pearl gray
359	801	Dark coffee brown
944	869	Very dark hazelnut brown
881	945	Tawny
1010	951	Light tawny
1030	3746	Dark blue violet
1032	3752	Very light antique blue
1031	3753	Ultra very light antique blue
140	3755	Baby blue
901	3829	Very dark old gold
9159	3841	Pale baby blue

FULL, HALF & QUARTER CROSS-STITCH (1X)

KREINIK VERY FINE (#4) BRAID		COLOR
028	m	Citron

BACKSTITCH & STRAIGHT STITCH (1X)

ANCHOR	DMC	COLORS
403	310	Black*
9046	321	Red*
973	3818	Ultra very dark emerald green

KREINIK VERY FINE (#4) BRAID	COLORS
028	Citron*

FRENCH KNOT (2X)

ANCHOR	DMC	COLORS
403	310	Black*
9046	321	Red*

ATTACH BEAD

MILL HILL GLASS SEED	COLOR
G00557	Old gold

*Duplicate color

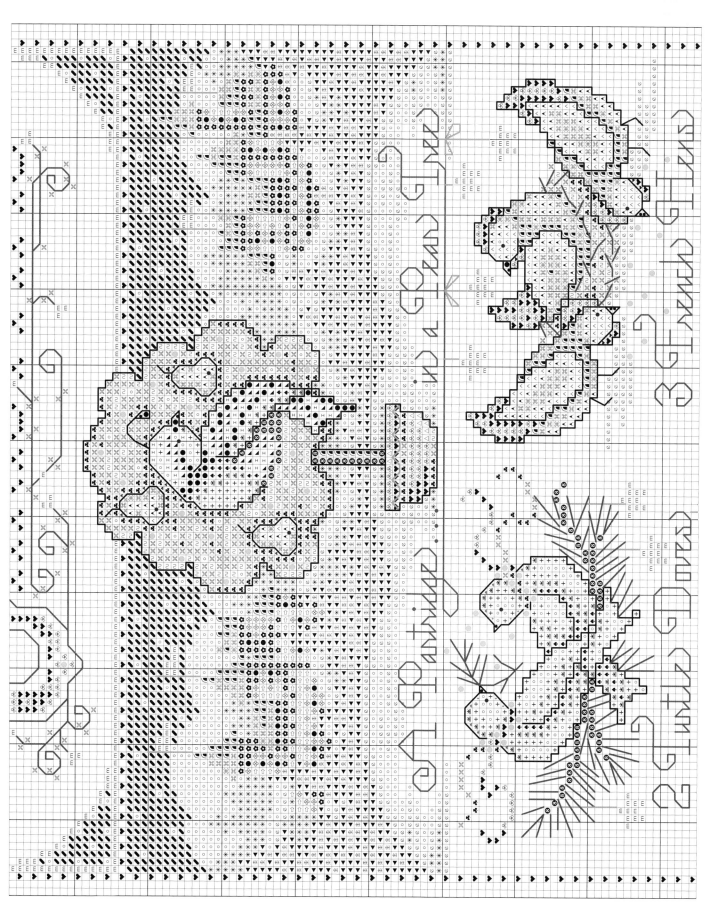

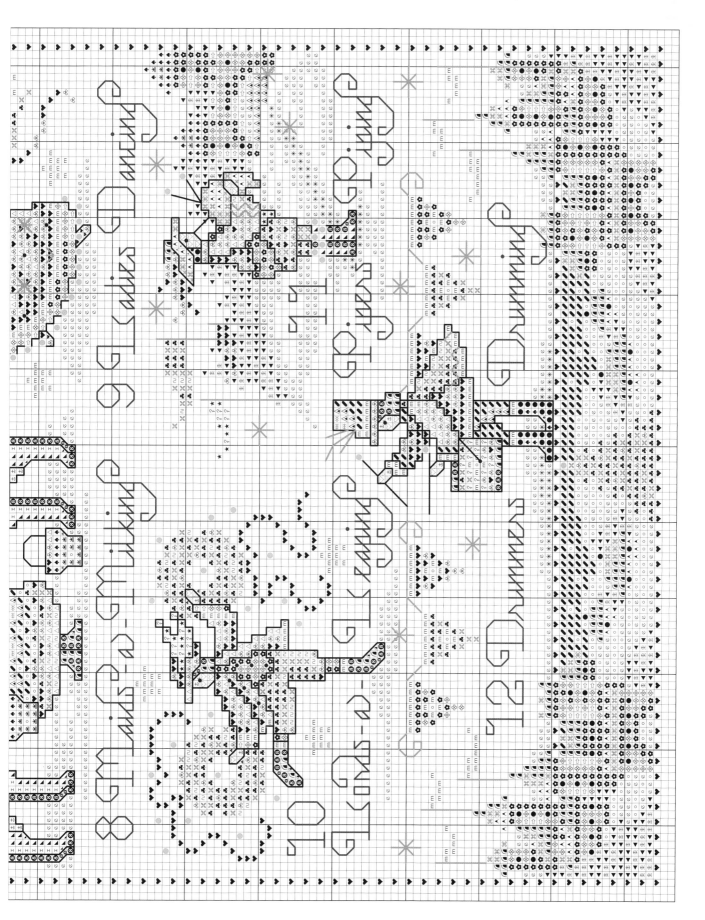

Christmas Stockings

Oh what fun it will be on Christmas morning when your precious little ones find their stockings filled with goodies from Santa. Stitch up these stockings and create an heirloom to cherish.

Materials for Each
- Blue blizzard 14-count Aida:
    15 x 20 inches
- DMC floss as indicated in color key
- Kreinik Fine (#4) Braid as indicated in color key
- 9 x 13 inches fusible fleece
- ½ yard fabric (for stocking and lining)
- 40 inches decorative braid
- Matching sewing thread
- Permanent fabric glue

    Dragon Stocking and Fairy Stocking were stitched on blue blizzard 14-count Aida from Wichelt using DMC floss and Kreinik braid.

Skill Level
Experienced

Stitch Count
100 wide x 160 high

Approximate Design Size
11-count 9" x 14½"
14-count 7⅛" x 11⅜"
16-count 6¼" x 10"
18-count 5½" x 8⅞"
25-count 4" x 6⅜"
28-count over 2 threads 7⅛" x 11⅜"
32-count over 2 threads 6¼" x 10"

Project Notes
Materials and finishing instructions are for stockings stitched on 14-count fabric or on 28-count fabric over two threads.

Stitching and finishing instructions are given on pages 20 and 21. An alphabet chart is included on page 20 for personalization.

Dragon Christmas Stocking

FULL, HALF & QUARTER CROSS-STITCH (2X)

ANCHOR		DMC	COLORS
2	o	1	White
109	a	155	Medium dark blue violet
403	●	310	Black
9046	♥	321	Red
119	✿	333	Very dark blue violet
46	✳	666	Bright red
891	☆	676	Light old gold
886	◇	677	Very light old gold
923	♣	699	Green
228	✚	700	Bright green
226	∽	702	Kelly green
238	e	703	Chartreuse
890	⌘	729	Medium old gold
303	★	742	Light tangerine
302	◉	743	Medium yellow
301	⟩	744	Pale yellow
132	♠	797	Royal blue
131	☺	798	Dark delft blue
136	⇨	799	Medium delft blue
944	⬅	869	Very dark hazelnut brown
881	✾	945	Tawny
1010	໑	951	Light tawny
25	♡	3716	Very light dusty rose
1030	▲	3746	Dark blue violet
1032	⋈	3752	Very light antique blue
1031	/	3753	Ultra very light antique blue
1098	⋘	3801	Light red
901	◣	3829	Very dark old gold

FULL, HALF & QUARTER CROSS-STITCH (1X)

KREINIK VERY FINE (#4) BRAID		COLORS
025	◆◆	Gray
028	m	Citron

BACKSTITCH (1X)

ANCHOR		DMC	COLORS
403	—	310	Black*
9046	—	321	Red*
923	—	699	Green*
136	—	799	Medium delft blue*

KREINIK VERY FINE (#4) BRAID		COLORS
025	—	Gray*
028	—	Citron*

FRENCH KNOT (2X)

ANCHOR		DMC	COLOR
403	●	310	Black*

FRENCH KNOT (1X)

KREINIK VERY FINE (#4) BRAID		COLOR
028	●	Citron*

*Duplicate color

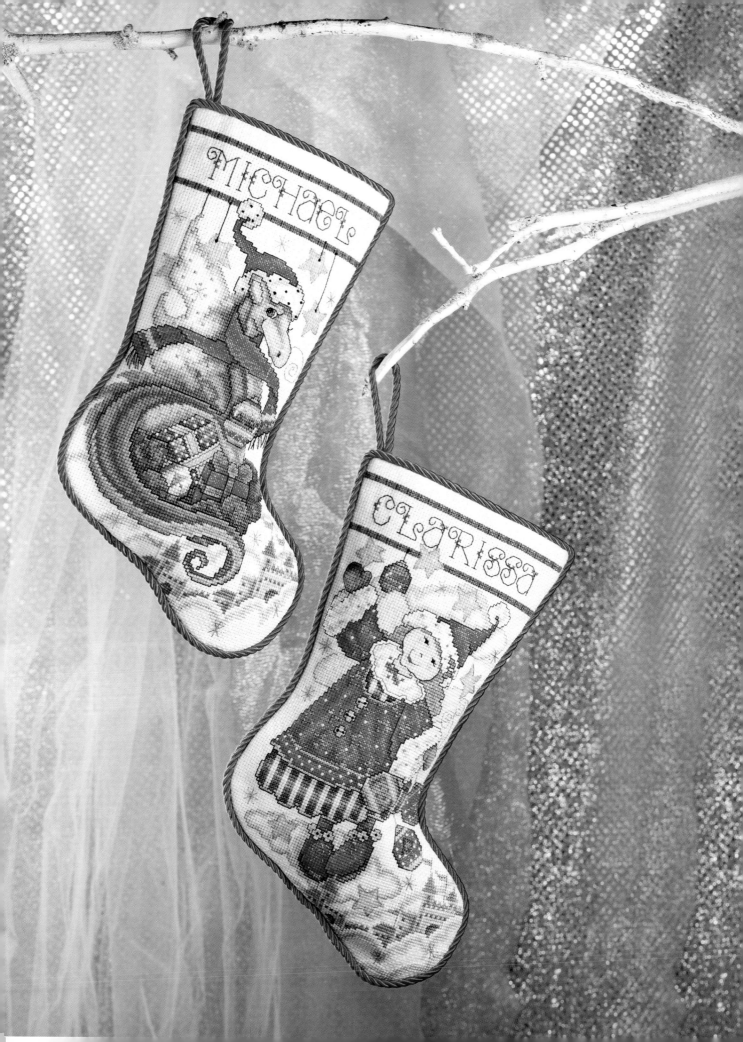

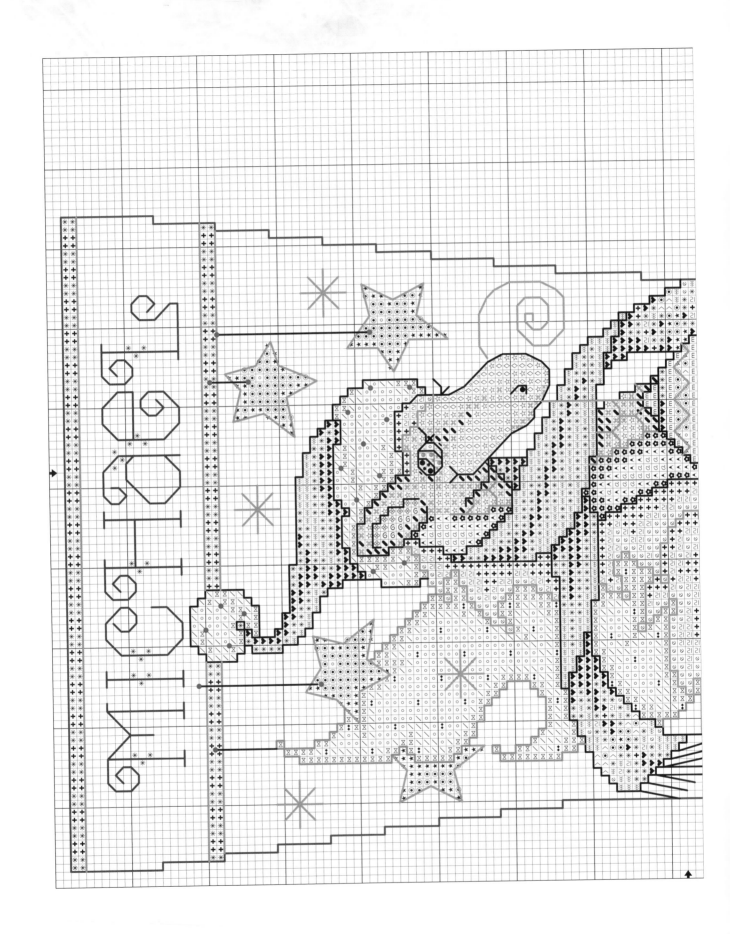

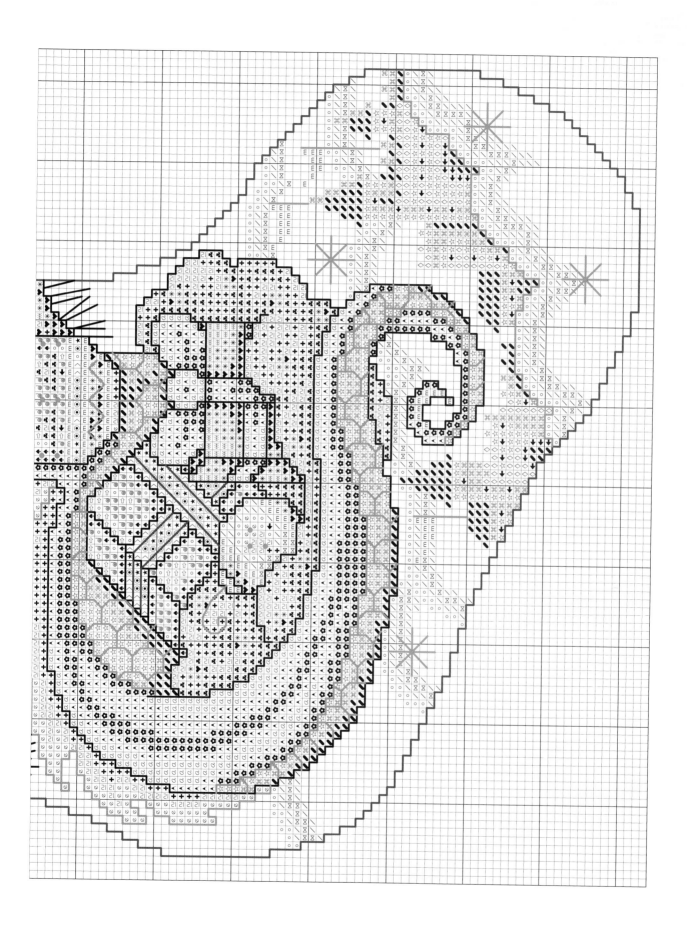

Christmas Stocking Alphabet Chart

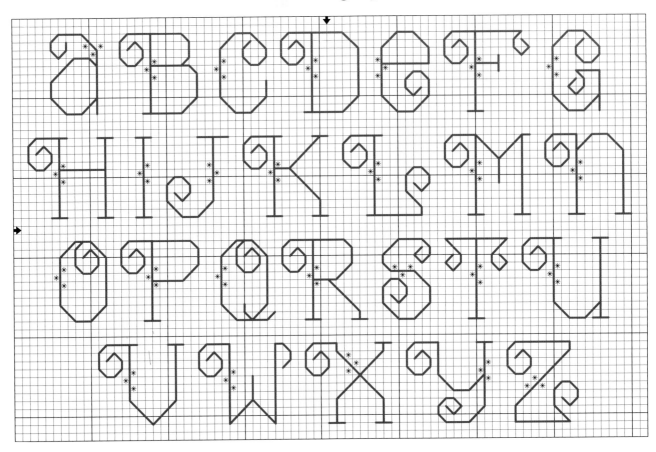

Stitching

Note: *Do not backstitch the red lines around the design. Baste along these lines as a guide for the final stocking shape and remove them afterward.*

Center and stitch each design on fabric using 2 strands floss or 1 strand Kreinik braid for full, half and quarter Cross-Stitch; 1 strand floss or Kreinik braid for Backstitch and lettering; and 2 strands floss or 1 strand Kreinik braid, wrapped once, for French Knot.

Stocking

Note: *Use ½-inch seam allowance throughout.*

1. Place 9 x 13-inch piece of fusible fleece on the wrong side of finished embroidery piece, covering red basting lines. Fuse according to manufacturer's instructions.

2. Cut out stocking shape ½ inch beyond red basting lines and 1 inch beyond the top edge of the design. Fold the top edge to the back ½ inch and press. Remove basting threads.

3. From ½ yard fabric, cut two 10 x 16-inch pieces; place right sides together. Center stocking shape on fabric; cut fabric to stocking shape, leaving 4 inches additional fabric at top.

4. Layer cut pieces as follows: fabric, right side up; embroidery design, right side up; and fabric, wrong side up. Pin together with bottom and side edges even.

5. Sew around sides and bottom of stocking, leaving a small opening for tucking in ends of decorative braid. Finish top raw edge of fabric by folding ½ inch to the wrong side and stitching. Turn stocking right side out.

6. For hanging loop, cut an 8-inch length of decorative braid. Fold in half and slip ends between embroidery design and fabric at left top corner. Hand-stitch the fabric to the folded top edge of the embroidery, catching ends of decorative braid in stitching.

7. Use permanent fabric glue to adhere remaining decorative braid around outer edge of stocking, tucking the ends into the bottom opening. Hand-stitch opening closed.

Fairy Christmas Stocking

FULL, HALF & QUARTER CROSS-STITCH (2X)

ANCHOR		DMC	COLORS
2	○	1	White
403	●	310	Black
9046	♥	321	Red
398	?	415	Pearl gray
46	✳	666	Bright red
891	☆	676	Light old gold
886	◇	677	Very light old gold
923	♣	699	Green
228	✤	700	Bright green
226	∿	702	Kelly green
238	e	703	Chartreuse
890	⌘	729	Medium old gold
303	★	742	Light tangerine
302	⊙	743	Medium yellow
301	⟩	744	Pale yellow
300	◁	745	Light pale yellow
234	∪	762	Very light pearl gray
132	♠	797	Royal blue
131	⌀	798	Dark delft blue
136	⇨	799	Medium delft blue
944	◀	869	Very dark hazelnut brown
881	⬡	945	Tawny
1010	∽	951	Light tawny
25	♡	3716	Very light dusty rose
1032	⋈	3752	Very light antique blue
1031	/	3753	Ultra very light antique blue
1098	⫝	3801	Light red
901	◢	3829	Very dark old gold

FULL, HALF & QUARTER CROSS-STITCH (1X)

KREINIK VERY FINE (#4) BRAID		COLOR
028	m	Citron

BACKSTITCH (1X)

ANCHOR	DMC	COLORS
403	310	Black*
9046	321	Red*
923	699	Green*
136	799	Medium delft blue*

KREINIK VERY FINE (#4) BRAID		COLOR
028	—	Citron*

FRENCH KNOT (2X)

ANCHOR	DMC	COLOR
403	310	Black*

FRENCH KNOT (1X)

KREINIK VERY FINE (#4) BRAID		COLOR
028	●	Citron*

*Duplicate color

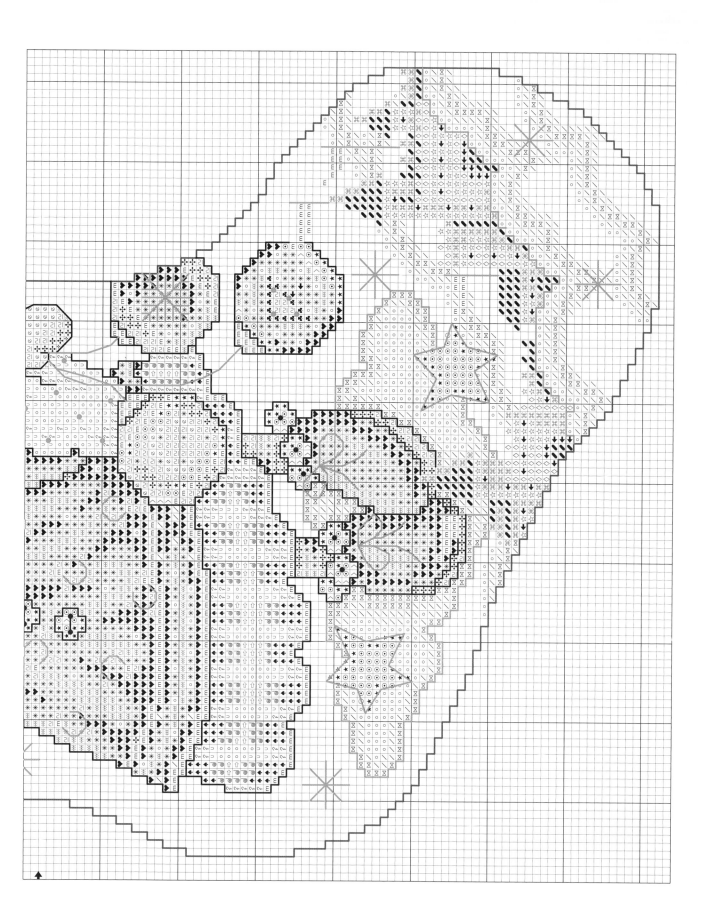

The Snow Princess

In the hush of the winter forest you can hear the soft rustling of her rich velvet skirt as the Snow Princess glides silently through the newly fallen snow. A crown of Christmas roses and sparkling snowflakes highlight her message of peace.

Materials

- Snowstorm 14- or 28-count Jobelan*:
  19 x 22 inches
- DMC floss as indicated in color key
- Kreinik Fine (#4) Braid as indicated in color key
- Mill Hill glass seed beads as indicated in color key

*The Snow Princess was stitched on snowstorm 28-count hand-dyed Jobelan from Polstitches Designs using DMC floss, Kreinik braid and Mill Hill glass seed beads. Finished piece was custom framed.

Skill Level

Experienced

Stitch Count

157 wide x 188 high

Approximate Design Size

11-count 14¼" x 17"
14-count 11¼" x 13⅜"
16-count 9⅞" x 11¾"
18-count 8¾" x 10⅜"
25-count 6¼" x 6½"
28-count over 2 threads 11¼" x 13⅜"
32-count over 2 threads 9⅞" x 11¾"

Stitching

Center and stitch design on fabric using 2 strands floss or 1 strand Kreinik braid for full, half and quarter Cross-Stitch; 1 strand floss or Kreinik braid for Backstitch; and 2 strands floss or Kreinik braid, wrapped once, for French Knot. Attach beads using 1 strand matching floss.

FULL, HALF & QUARTER CROSS-STITCH (2X)

ANCHOR		DMC	COLORS
2	o	1	White
120	◿	157	Very light cornflower blue
400	❋	317	Pewter gray
399	?	318	Light steel gray
398	=	415	Pearl gray
374	⌘	420	Dark hazelnut brown
943	✓	422	Light hazelnut brown
891	⍭	676	Light old gold
886	☆	677	Very light old gold
890	⇨	729	Medium old gold
275	«	746	Off-white
941	←	792	Dark cornflower blue
176	◭	793	Medium cornflower blue
175	I	794	Light cornflower blue
944	✿	869	Very dark hazelnut brown
1033	▲	932	Light antique blue
881	◢	945	Tawny
1010	✤	951	Light tawny
1001	✖	976	Medium golden brown
871	◆◆	3041	Medium antique violet
870	⬡	3042	Light antique violet
262	✖	3363	Medium pine green
260	⏛	3364	Pine green
68	e	3687	Mauve
873	◣	3740	Dark antique violet
869	V	3743	Very light antique violet
1032	S	3752	Very light antique blue
1031	□	3753	Ultra very light antique blue
1009	⎗	3770	Very light tawny
236	❽	3799	Very dark pewter gray
877	♣	3815	Dark celadon green
876	±	3816	Medium celadon green
875	a	3817	Light celadon green
1049	◆	3826	Golden brown
901	★	3829	Very dark old gold

FULL, HALF & QUARTER CROSS-STITCH (1X)

KREINIK VERY FINE (#4) BRAID		COLORS
002	@	Gold
102	m	Vatican gold

BACKSTITCH & STRAIGHT STITCH (1X)

ANCHOR		DMC	COLORS
944	—	869	Very dark hazelnut brown* (eyebrow)
236	—	3799	Very dark pewter gray* (princess, skirt, shoe, animals)
972	—	3803	Medium mauve (lips)

KREINIK VERY FINE (#4) BRAID		COLORS
002	—	Gold* (flowers, twig)
102	—	Vatican gold* (snowflakes, skirt ruffle)

FRENCH KNOT (2X)

ANCHOR		DMC	COLOR
236	●	3799	Very dark pewter gray*

KREINIK VERY FINE (#4) BRAID		COLOR
002	●	Gold* (sleeves)

ATTACH BEAD

MILL HILL GLASS SEED		COLORS
G00557	●	Gold
G02010	●	Ice

*Duplicate color

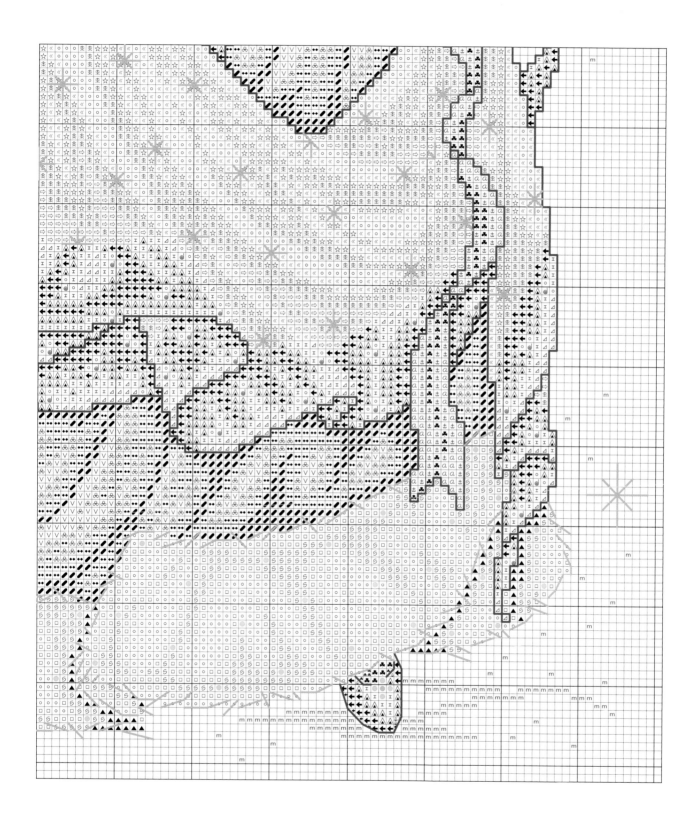

Redwork Christmas Samplers

The simple beauty of classic redwork is perfectly suited for your holiday stitching. These pretty little samplers stitch up so quickly and will make lovely handmade gifts. Silhouettes of Christmas trees, snowflakes, gentle doves and holiday homes all combine in a tribute to the wonderful Christmas traditions we cherish.

Materials for Each
- White 14-count Aida*:
    13 x 15 inches
- DMC floss as indicated in color key

   Redwork Christmas Samplers were stitched on white 14-count Aida from Wichelt using DMC floss. Finished pieces were custom framed.

Skill Level
Easy

Stitch Count
69 wide x 97 high

Approximate Design Size
11-count 6¼" x 8⅞"
14-count 5" x 7"
16-count 4⅜" x 6"
18-count 3⅞" x 5⅜"
25-count 2¾" x 3⅞"
28-count over 2 threads 5" x 7"
32-count over 2 threads 4⅜" x 6"

Project Note
Create your own variations of the redwork samplers by mixing and matching the motifs and adding personalization with the alphabet.

Stitching
Center and stitch design on fabric using 2 strands floss for full Cross-Stitch and 1 strand floss for Backstitch.

FULL, HALF & QUARTER CROSS-STITCH (2X)

ANCHOR		DMC	COLOR
9046	♥	321	Red

BACKSTITCH (1X)

ANCHOR		DMC	COLOR
9046	▬	321	Red*

*Duplicate color

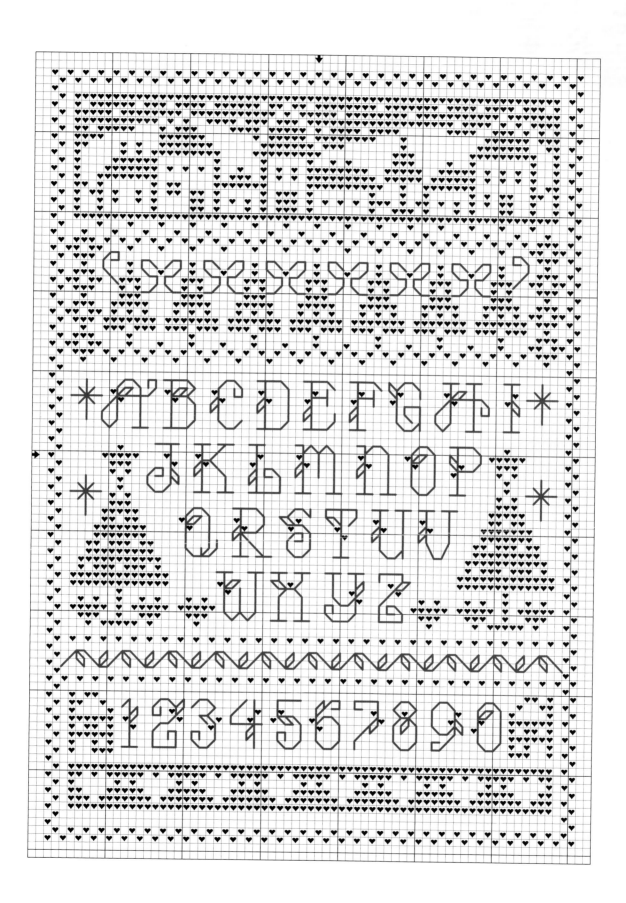

Snow Much Fun

Five frolicking snowmen dressed in their cozy winter scarves and hats are all abuzz getting the tree ready for the holidays. The boxes of shiny decorations and strings of colorful lights are down from the attic and ready to go. Come join in as everyone does their part to make this festive Christmas scene a fun time for all.

Materials

- Blue blizzard opalescent 14- or 28-count Aida*:
    18 x 16 inches
- DMC floss as indicated in color key
- Kreinik Fine (#4) Braid as indicated in color key

  Snow Much Fun was stitched on blue blizzard opalescent 28-count Aida from Wichelt using DMC floss and Kreinik braid. Finished piece was custom framed.

Skill Level

Easy

Stitch Count

140 wide x 112 high

Approximate Design Size

11-count 12¾" x 10⅛"
14-count 10" x 8"
16-count 8¾" x 7"
18-count 7¾" x 6¼"
25-count 5⅝" x 4½"
28-count over 2 threads 10" x 8"
32-count over 2 threads 8¾" x 7"

Stitching

Center and stitch design on fabric using 2 strands floss or 1 strand Kreinik braid for full, half and quarter Cross-Stitch; 2 strands floss for Backstitch on snowmen arms; 1 strand floss or Kreinik braid for all remaining Backstitch; and 2 strands floss, wrapped once, for French Knot.

FULL, HALF & QUARTER CROSS-STITCH (2X)

ANCHOR		DMC	COLORS
2	○	1	White
403	●	310	Black
399	◪	318	Light steel gray
9046	♥	321	Red
398	∩	415	Pearl gray
46	✛	666	Bright red
228	♣	700	Bright green
226	≈	702	Kelly green
238	△	703	Chartreuse
304	✿	741	Medium tangerine
303	★	742	Light tangerine
302	?	743	Medium yellow
301	<	744	Pale yellow
234	∞	762	Very light pearl gray
132	➡	797	Royal blue
131	✳	798	Dark delft blue
136	V	799	Medium delft blue
25	♡	3716	Very light dusty rose
1098	⫷	3801	Light red
901	◆◆	3829	Very dark old gold

FULL, HALF & QUARTER CROSS-STITCH (1X)

KREINIK VERY FINE (#4) BRAID		COLOR
028	m	Citron

BACKSTITCH (2X)

ANCHOR		DMC	COLOR
403	—	310	Black* (snowman arms)

BACKSTITCH (1X)

ANCHOR		DMC	COLORS
403	—	310	Black* (all remaining black outlines)
9046	—	321	Red*
228	—	700	Bright green*

KREINIK VERY FINE (#4) BRAID		COLOR
028	—	Citron*

FRENCH KNOT (2X)

ANCHOR		DMC	COLOR
403	●	310	Black*

*Duplicate color

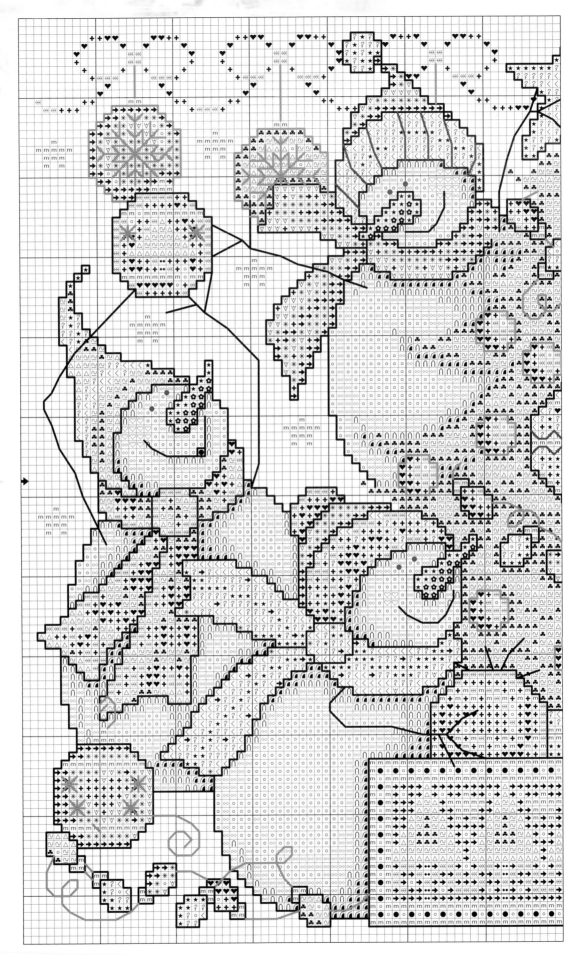

Christmas Greetings

Get ready for a jolly Christmas with Santa and his charming North Pole friends! Send a bit of holiday cheer with hand-stitched cards and gift bags made especially for those nearest and dearest to your heart. These fun and festive cards will bring a smile to their faces and warm their hearts with cheerful Christmas greetings.

Materials for Each
- Silver stardust 14-count Aida*:
    8 x 10 inches
- DMC floss as indicated in color key
- Kreinik Fine (#4) Braid as indicated in color key

Additional Materials for Each Card
- 8 x 8-inch piece cardstock
- Double-sided tape
- Desired winter-themed embellishments

Additional Materials for Each Gift Bag
- 9 x 12-inch piece red craft felt
- Matching all-purpose thread
- Pinking shears (optional)
- 3 x 8-inch piece of fusible web
- 18 inches ¼-inch-wide green ribbon

*Christmas Greetings were stitched on silver stardust 14-count Aida from Charlescraft using DMC floss and Kreinik braid.

Skill Level
Easy

Stitch Count
36 wide x 90 high

Approximate Design Size
11-count 3¼" x 8⅛"
14-count 2½" x 6½"
16-count 2¼" x 5⅝"
18-count 2" x 5"
25-count 1⅜" x 3⅝"
28-count over 2 threads 2½" x 6½"
32-count over 2 threads 2¼" x 5⅝"

Project Note
Materials and finishing instructions are for designs stitched on 14-count fabric or on 28-count fabric stitching over 2 threads.

Stitching
Center and stitch design on fabric using 2 strands floss or 1 strand Kreinik braid for full and quarter Cross-Stitch; 1 strand floss or Kreinik braid for Backstitch; and 2 strands floss, wrapped once, for French Knot.

Greeting Card
1. Fold cardstock in half to make a 4 x 8-inch, side-fold card.
2. Trim stitched piece four rows beyond stitching all around. Pull out the last two rows of Aida to create a fringed edge. Center stitched piece on front of card and adhere with double-sided tape.
4. Embellish as desired.

Gift Bag
1. Cut felt in half to create two 4½ x 12-inch pieces. Layer pieces with edges even.
2. Using a ½-inch seam allowance, sew down both long edges and across the bottom edge. If desired, embellish edges with pinking shears.
3. Trim stitched piece four rows beyond stitching all around. Pull out last two rows of Aida to create a fringe.
4. Cut a piece of fusible web the same size as the trimmed stitching.
5. Center stitched piece on front of bag, sandwiching fusible web between. Press to fuse.
6. Gather top of bag closed and tie with ribbon.

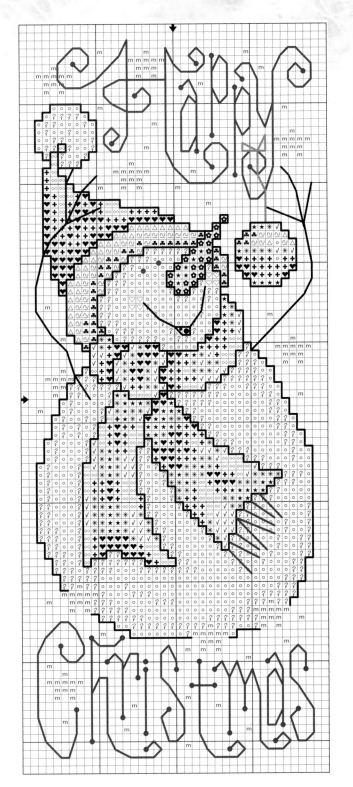

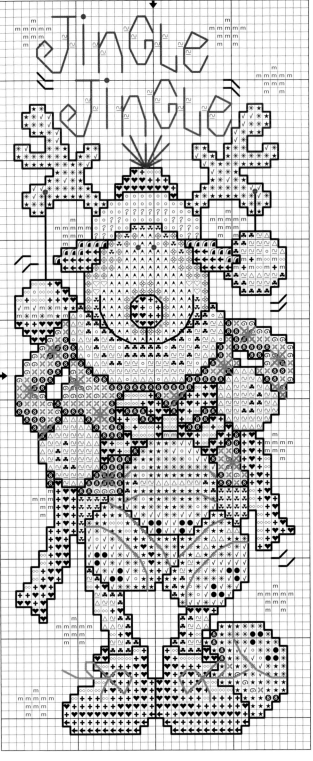

FULL, HALF & QUARTER CROSS-STITCH (2X)

ANCHOR		DMC	COLORS
2	o	1	White
403	●	310	Black
1017	◣	318	Light steel gray
9046	♥	321	Red
398	?	415	Pearl gray
46	✚	666	Bright red
391	▲	676	Light old gold
228	♣	700	Bright green

ANCHOR		DMC	COLORS
226	∽	702	Kelly green
238	△	703	Chartreuse
890	✿	729	Medium old gold
304	✿	741	Medium tangerine
303	★	742	Light tangerine
302	✱	743	Medium yellow
301	√	744	Pale yellow
132	⑧	797	Royal blue
131	✕	798	Dark delft blue

ANCHOR		DMC	COLORS
136	⌐	799	Medium delft blue
359	◀	801	Dark coffee brown
944	◖	869	Very dark hazelnut brown
881	◔	945	Tawny
1010	✛	951	Light tawny
25	♡	3716	Very light dusty rose
1098	◇◇	3801	Light red
901	▼	3829	Very dark old gold

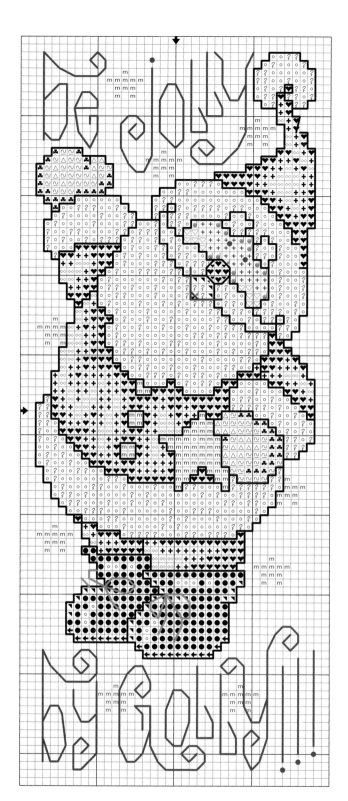

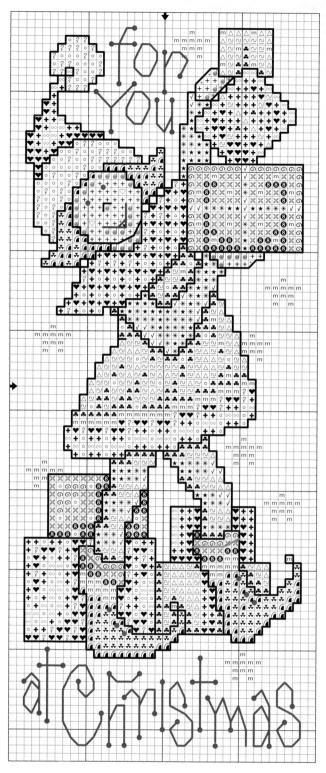

BACKSTITCH (1X)

ANCHOR	DMC	COLORS
403	310	Black*
9046	321	Red*
228	700	Bright green*

KREINIK VERY
FINE (#4) BRAID COLOR
028 Citron*

FULL, HALF & QUARTER CROSS-STITCH (1X)

KREINIK VERY
FINE (#4) BRAID COLOR
028 [m] Citron

FRENCH KNOT (2X)

ANCHOR	DMC	COLORS
403	310	Black*
9046	321	Red*
228	700	Bright green*

*Duplicate color

Christmas Roly-Polies

Ho, ho, ho and Merry Christmas! It's time to trim the tree and deck the halls. These delightful ornaments will make a lovely addition to your holiday decorations. So come join in with Santa and Mrs. Claus and all their happy holiday friends to make this the merriest Christmas ever.

Mrs. Claus Stitch Count
43 wide x 51 high

Mrs. Claus Approximate Design Size
10-count 4⅜" x 5⅛"
14-count 3" x 3⅝"

Santa Stitch Count
42 wide x 52 high

Santa Approximate Design Size
10-count 4¼" x 5¼"
14-count 3" x 3¾"

Snowman Stitch Count
41 wide x 52 high

Snowman Approximate Design Size
10-count 4⅛" x 5¼"
14-count 3" x 3¾"

Materials for Each Ornament

- Clear 14-count plastic canvas*:
  ½ sheet
- DMC floss as indicated in color key
- Kreinik Fine (#4) Braid as indicated in color key
- 9 x 12-inch sheet self-adhesive craft felt
- 9 inches ⅛-inch-wide red ribbon
- Small, sharp scissors

  Christmas Roly-Polies were stitched on clear 14-count plastic canvas using DMC floss and Kreinik braid.

Skill Level
Easy

Stitching

Center and stitch design on plastic canvas using 2 strands floss or 1 strand Kreinik braid for full Cross-Stitch; 1 strand floss or Kreinik braid for Backstitch; and 2 strands floss, wrapped once, for French Knot.

Ornaments

1. Adhere felt to back of stitched piece.
2. Using small, sharp scissors, carefully cut out ornament, leaving one bar beyond stitching.
3. Cut a 9-inch length of red ribbon. Insert through center top of ornament and tie into a hanging loop.

Angel Stitch Count
43 wide x 51 high

Angel Approximate Design Size
10-count 4⅜" x 5⅛"
14-count 3" x 3⅝"

Penguin Stitch Count
42 wide x 52 high

Penguin Approximate Design Size
10-count 4¼" x 5¼"
14-count 3" x 3¾"

Bear Stitch Count
42 wide x 51 high

Bear Approximate Design Size
10-count 4¼" x 5⅛"
14-count 3" x 3⅝"

FULL, HALF & QUARTER CROSS-STITCH (2X)

ANCHOR		DMC	COLORS
2	○	1	White
403	●	310	Black
399	◪	318	Light steel gray
9046	♥	321	Red
398	∩	415	Pearl gray
46	✛	666	Bright red
891	◉	676	Light old gold
228	♣	700	Bright green
226	∾	702	Kelly green
238	V	703	Chartreuse
890	⫸	729	Medium old gold
304	★	741	Medium tangerine
303	▲	742	Light tangerine
302	✳	743	Medium yellow
301	I	744	Pale yellow
275	≪	746	Off-white
132	←	797	Royal blue
131	⊞	798	Dark delft blue
136	⇨	799	Medium delft blue
881	╋	945	Tawny
1010	e	951	Light tawny
25	♡	3716	Very light dusty rose
1098	⋈	3801	Light red
901	✿	3829	Very dark old gold

FULL, HALF & QUARTER CROSS-STITCH (1X)

KREINIK VERY FINE (#4) BRAID		COLOR
028	m	Citron

BACKSTITCH (1X)

ANCHOR		DMC	COLORS
2	▬	1	White* (gingerbread man)
403	▬	310	Black*
9046	▬	321	Red*

KREINIK VERY FINE (#4) BRAID		COLOR
028	▬	Citron*

FRENCH KNOT (2X)

ANCHOR		DMC	COLORS
403	●	310	Black*
9046	●	321	Red*

KREINIK VERY FINE (#4) BRAID		COLOR
028	●	Citron*

*Duplicate color

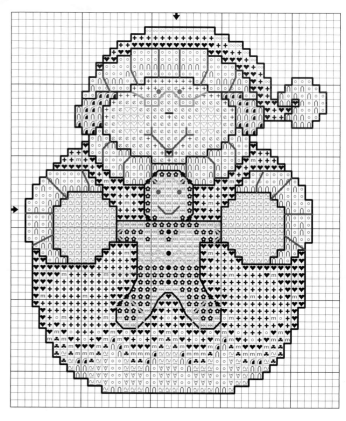

How to Stitch

Working From Charted Designs

A square on a chart corresponds to a space for a Cross-Stitch on the stitching surface. The symbol in a square shows the floss color to be used for the stitch. The width and height for the design stitch-area are given; centers are shown by arrows. Backstitches are shown by straight lines, and French Knots are shown by dots.

Fabrics

In our Materials listings we give Joan Elliott's fabric suggestions that will complement each design. Our stitched models were worked on 14- and 28-count evenweave fabric that has the same number of horizontal and vertical threads (or blocks of threads) per inch. That number is called the thread count.

The size of the design is determined by the size of the evenweave fabric on which you work. Use the chart below as a guide to determine the finished size of a design on various popular sizes of cross-stitch fabric.

Thread	Number of Stitches in Design				
Count	10	20	30	40	50
11-count	1"	1¾"	2¾"	3⅝"	4½"
14-count	¾"	1⅜"	2⅛"	2⅞"	3⅝"
16-count	⅝"	1¼"	1⅞"	2½"	3⅛"
18-count	½"	1⅛"	1⅝"	2¼"	2¾"
25-count	⅜"	⅞"	1¼"	1⅝"	2"
28-count	⅜"	¾"	1"	1⅜"	1¾"
32-count	¼"	⅝"	⅞"	1¼"	1½"

(measurements are given to the nearest ⅛")

Needles

A blunt-tipped tapestry needle, size 24 or 26, is used for stitching on most 14-count to 28-count fabrics. The higher the needle number, the smaller the needle. The correct-size needle is easy to thread with the amount of floss required, but is not so large that it will distort the holes in the fabric. The following chart indicates the appropriate-size needle for each size of fabric, along with the suggested number of strands of floss to use.

Fabric	Strands of Floss	Tapestry Needle Size
11-count	3	24 or 26
14-count	2	24 or 26
16-count	2	24, 26 or 28
18-count	1 or 2	26 or 28
25-count	1	26 or 28
28-count over two threads	2	26 or 28
32-count over two threads	2	28

Floss

All of our models were stitched using DMC six-strand embroidery floss. Color numbers are given for floss. Both DMC and Anchor color numbers are given for each design. Cut floss into comfortable working lengths; we suggest about 18 inches.

Blending Filament & Metallic Braid

Blending filament is a fine, shiny fiber that can be used alone or combined with floss or other thread. Knotting the blending filament on the needle with a slip knot is recommended for control (Fig. 1).

Fig. 1
Slip Knot

Metallic braid is a braided metallic fiber, usually used single-ply. Thread this fiber just as you would any other fiber. Use short lengths, about 15 inches, to keep the fiber from fraying.

Getting Started

To begin in an unstitched area, bring threaded needle from back to front of fabric. Hold an inch of the end against the back, and then hold it in place with your first few stitches. To end threads and begin new ones next to existing stitches, weave through the backs of several stitches.

The Stitches

The number of strands used for Cross-Stitches will be determined by the thread count of the fabric used. Refer to the needles chart to determine the number of strands used for Cross-Stitches. Use one strand for Backstitches.

Cross-Stitch

The Cross-Stitch is formed in two motions. Follow the numbering in Fig. 2 and bring needle up at 1, down at 2, up at 3 and down at 4 to complete the stitch. Work horizontal rows of stitches (Fig. 3) wherever possible. Bring thread up at 1, work half of each stitch across the row, and then complete the stitches on your return.

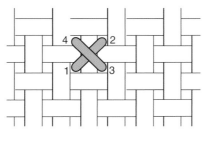

Fig. 2
Cross-Stitch

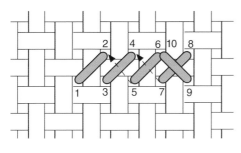

Fig. 3
Cross-Stitch
Horizontal Row

Half Cross-Stitch

The first part of a Cross-Stitch may slant in either direction (Fig. 4).

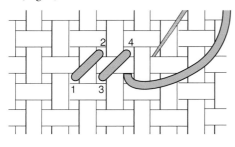

Fig. 4
Half Cross-Stitch

Quarter Cross-Stitch

The Quarter Cross-Stitch is formed in one motion. Follow the numbering in Fig. 5 and bring needle up at 1 and down at 2. The Quarter Cross-Stitch is used to fill in small spaces in the design where there is not enough room for a full stitch.

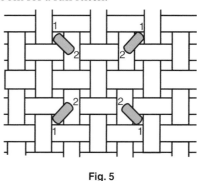

Fig. 5
Quarter Cross-Stitch

Backstitch

Backstitches are worked after Cross-Stitches have been completed. They may slope in any direction and are occasionally worked over more than one square of fabric. Fig. 6 shows the progression of several stitches; bring thread up at odd numbers and down at even numbers. Frequently, you must choose where to end one Backstitch color and begin the next color. Choose the object that should appear closest to you. Backstitch around that shape with the appropriate color, and then Backstitch the areas behind it with adjacent color(s).

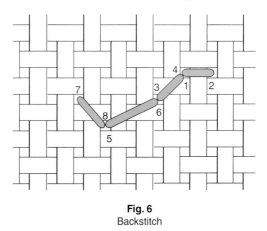

Fig. 6
Backstitch

French Knot

Bring thread up where indicated on chart. Wrap floss once around needle (Fig. 7) and reinsert needle at 2, close to 1 but at least one fabric thread away from it. Hold wrapping thread tightly and pull needle through, letting thread go just as knot is formed. For a larger knot, use more strands of floss.

Fig. 7
French Knot

Stitching With Beads

Small seed beads can be added to any cross-stitch design, using one bead per stitch. Knot thread at beginning of beaded section for security, especially if you are adding beads to clothing. The bead should lie in the same direction as the top half of cross-stitches.

Bead Attachment

Use one strand of floss to secure beads. Bring beading needle up from back of work (Fig. 8), leaving a 2-inch length of thread hanging; do not knot (end will be secured between stitches as you work). Thread bead on needle; complete stitch.

Do not skip over more than two stitches or spaces without first securing thread, or last bead will be loose. To secure, weave thread into several stitches on back of work. Follow graph to work design, using one bead per stitch.

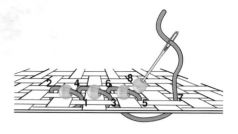

Fig. 8
Bead Attachment

Planning a Project

Before you stitch, decide how large to cut fabric. Determine the stitched size and then allow enough additional fabric around the design plus 4 inches more on each side for use in finishing and mounting.

Cut your fabric exactly true, right along the holes of the fabric. Some raveling may occur as you handle the fabric. To minimize raveling along the raw edges, use an overcast basting stitch, machine zigzag-stitch or masking tape, which you can cut away when you are finished.

Finishing Needlework

When you have finished stitching, dampen your embroidery (or, if soiled, wash in lukewarm mild soapsuds and rinse well). Roll in a towel to remove excess moisture. Place facedown on a dry towel or padded surface; press carefully until dry and smooth. Make sure all thread ends are well anchored and clipped closely. Proceed with desired finishing.

Annie's®

Christmas Cross-Stitch Treasures is published by Annie's, 306 East Parr Road, Berne, IN 46711. Printed in USA. Copyright © 2013 Annie's.

RETAIL STORES: If you would like to carry this publication or any other Annie's publications, visit AnniesWSL.com.

Every effort has been made to ensure that the instructions in this pattern book are complete and accurate. We cannot, however, take responsibility for human error, typographical mistakes or variations in individual work. Please visit AnniesCustomerCare.com to check for pattern updates.

STAFF

Editor: Barb Sprunger
Publishing Services Director: Brenda Gallmeyer
Copy Supervisor: Corene Painter
Senior Copy Editor: Emily Carter
Copy Editor: Samantha Mawhorter
Production Artist Supervisor: Erin Brandt
Senior Production Artist: Nicole Gage

Production Artist: Amanda Treharn
Creative Director: Brad Snow
Graphic Designer: Nick Pierce
Photography Supervisor: Tammy Christian
Photography: Matthew Owen
Photo Stylists: Tammy Liechty, Tammy Steiner

ISBN: 978-1-59635-749-5

1 2 3 4 5 6 7 8 9